Between Breaths

'breathing dreams like air'
(The Great Gatsby)

~ F. Scott Fitzgerald

Also by Jane Williams

Points of Recognition *Ginninderra Press 2021*
Parts of the Main *Ginninderra Press 2017*
Days Like These (selected and new poems) *Interactive Press 2013*
City of Possibilities *Interactive Press 2011*
Begging the Question *Ginninderra Press 2008*
Some Towns and other poems *Picaro Press in 2007*
The Last Tourist *Five Islands Press 2006*
Outside Temple Boundaries *Five Islands Press 1998*

Between Breaths

Jane Williams

Silver Bow Publishing
720 Sixth Street, Unit # 5
New Westminster, BC
CANADA V3L3C5

Title: Between Breaths
Author: Jane Williams
Cover Art: "Distant Sun" painting by Candice James
Layout and Design: Candice James
Editor: Candice James
ISBN:9781774031537 (print)
ISBN:9781774031544 (epub)

All rights reserved including the right to reproduce or translate this book or any portions thereof, in any form without the permission of the publisher. Except for the use of short passages for review purposes, no part of this book may be reproduced, in part or in whole, or transmitted in any form or by any means, electronically or mechanically, including photocopying, recording, or any information or storage retrieval system without prior permission in writing from the publisher or a licence from the Canadian Copyright Collective Agency (Access Copyright).

www.silverbowpublishing.com
info@silverbowpublishing.com
© Silver Bow Publishing 2021

Library and Archives Canada Cataloguing in Publication

Title: Between breaths / Jane Williams.
Names: Williams, Jane, 1964- author.
Description: Poems.
Identifiers: Canadiana (print) 2021015344X | Canadiana (ebook) 20210153474 | ISBN 9781774031537
   (softcover) | ISBN 9781774031544 (Kindle)
Classification: LCC PR9619.3.W5655 B48 2021 | DDC 821/.914—dc23

Between Breaths

For Ralph

Between Breaths

Acknowledgement

I wish to acknowledge with gratitude, Angela T. Carr for being instrumental in helping me break a writing drought of several months and find my groove again. Many of these poems were first drafted during Angela's online writing challenges, in the company of many fine poets.

Between Breaths

Contents

Stargazers ... 11
Year of the Rat ... 12
The Serendipity of Birds ... 13
Roget's Search for Meaning in 6 Parts ... 15
Flux ... 16
Traveling Through Winter ... 17
In This Photo I Am on the Cusp ... 18
The Word Itself ... 20
To the Householder ... 21
All Souls' Day ... 22
Liberty ... 24
Recalibration ... 26
Guises ... 27
Introductions ... 28
Fairy Tales from the Future ... 30
Incognito ... 31
The Lore of Poetry ... 32
Discovering Iris ... 33
What Hope Did We Have? ... 34
In His Way ... 35
Family Traits ... 36
Small Offerings ... 37
Though I Whispered Subliminal Poetry ... 38
To the Hitchhiker ... 39
Gold ... 40
In Hindsight ... 41
Milk Moon ... 42
Writing the Light ... 44
Meditation for the World Weary ... 45
Dog with Girl ... 46
How I Come to Know You ... 47
Some Thoughts in Red ... 49
Makers ... 50
The Ghost of Maria Goretti Speaks ... 52

Blooming in the Dark ... 53
The Other Side ... 54
Play ... 55
Today Was Inconsolable ... 56
The Spark ... 57
The Gap ... 58
Dream Analysis 101 ... 59
Redefining Romance ... 60
My Relationship with Food ... 61
Intuited ... 63
Out for the Count ... 64
No Thanks but in the Giving ... 65
Now You Think You Have Learned ... 67
This Prodigious Life ... 69

Author Profile ... 70

Stargazers

If there were such a thing
as the black box of genetic memory
looking inside might be like
unearthing the word *fernweh*
and feeling a sense of kinship toward
all that is believable but untranslatable.

This far-sickness must be the opposite
of nostalgia and more complicated
than pure escapism or déjà vu.

How can we not take it personally
to the extent the speed of light
has revealed us to ourselves.

How can we not venture forth,
dream we are standing at the edge
of the known universe looking down
into the windows of the souls of others,
their vaguely humanoid heads tilted
back up at us, stargazing...

Year of the Rat

For some, at first,
there must have been a degree of relief
to the days, to relationships sans touch.

Perhaps it was all they could do
not to prance about,
faces like singing kettles;
the pressure finally off
to kiss the proffered cheek
of fair-weathered friends,
clamp the newest colleague's
industrious palm...

all the while daydreaming
about claiming squatters' rights
to the impersonal
space between bodies.

For others,
the novelty of tapping elbows
and bumping hips
quickly thinned to gossamer
leaving a patina of small but indelible
skin-starved griefs.

Screen time became wholly qualitative,
oscillating between reruns of contact sport
and anything set in the wild.

Watching Macaque monkeys, stroke for stroke,
proved a particular source of comfort.

And for others, yet again, what could it mean
but more of the same? Another fissure in the divide
separating word from deed?
Hyperbole from the artless fundamentals of love?

The Serendipity of Birds

When was the first time I encountered them?

City doves perhaps, cooing through snowfall,
the push-pull of my birth day.
Their mixed heritage toughening constitutions,
negating migration.

Feeding ducks in park ponds with my father,
trying to jolly us both into the new world.

Moving *Down Under*
was I old enough to register
the shock of a black swan?
Decades later discovering
the term angel wing and its cruel irony.

I have become almost desensitised
to all manner of roadkill,
but then when I see a twist of crow on the tarmac
some ancient bell tolls its warning reminding me
adaptation and talent are no guarantee
of safe passage.

But this morning the doves find me again,
the pitying doves alighting from the bushes
and sweeping a single awesome circle
of air above my head,
before resuming their landlocked pecking order,
their pedestrian day.

And because of this
I am inclined toward the most speculative of potential
in my own species -
for each of us to recognise ourselves in the other,
reading mirrored signs with unchecked compassion:

This way up.
Handle with care.
Please do not bend.

To imagine the skies
filled once more with fledgling souls:
Mysterious Starlings.
Wonder Chickens.
Pagan Reed-warblers.

Even that earth-bound Dodo
could be dancing a dust bowl back to life
in some neighbouring dimension,
flapping its ill-proportioned wings,
hope against hope.

Roget's Search for Meaning in 6 Parts

Abstract
We cannot harness time.
The fascination of youth
and the shock of its decline
are merely distractions
from the work at hand.

Space
One can only walk around
inside the wardrobe
of oneself for so long
before suspecting everyone
of having a skeleton key.

Matter
There are family traits
which cannot be outgrown
but there is respite
in the catalogued life.

Intelligence
There are no
convincing words
for substitute.

Freewill
Some deceptions
are worth clinging to.

Sentience
Just in case
the anagram for dog
is more than happenstance
we must take great care
who we leave chained to the post
howling down moonbeams.

Flux

Try not to worry,
it is not something
you can plan for or guard against
(think of the oxymoron of a safety net).

For instance ...

One day the ocean morphed before my eyes
into a yellow flowering landscape.
I was so sure of its thingness
and could no more be frightened of it
than of my own selfhood.
It was as if I was glimpsing a time pre- and post-
I have long since given up trying to explain it.
Only that it happened somewhere
between grief and grief.

The night before my car broke down
smoke snaking from its engine like a resentful genie
I dreamt my car broke down, smoke snaking etc.
Ditto the night before my mother could not slake
her thirst or find her equilibrium and my father
thought she'd had a stroke, freeze-framing us all.

When my first-born grown up daughter tells me
her favourite dog is a Dalmatian,
I tell her when she was in utero
and all I could stomach was dry toast
and cups of weak tea,
a wasp swelled my arm to Michelin size
and a black and white spotted ghost dog appeared
and disappeared in the living room, asking for nothing.

Perhaps if we can accept anything about life
it is its potential to exceed all expectations.
We are in a sacred state of flux
which stops only when we do.

Traveling Through Winter

The world is shrinking from our touch,
our incessant calendaring.

How many true winters do we have left?

Memories like clouds of breath
fade even as they are formed –

Rescuing the snowed-in cat so he
could keep convincing us about love.

A mid-air mountain snowball electrifying
my sister's face, momentarily collapsing walls.

Watching ice float down the Danube
between countries, perfectly arrow-shaped.

Discovering how to stay warm on gyros
and Hungarian folk dancing.

Meeting a pen pal surreally in Chicago
by the ice-skating rink, tempted.

Wearing my daughter's faux leopard skin
earmuffs, unable not to think of her.

Photographing white swans
dreaming of black ones.

Teasing out 4% Icelandic from Ancestry DNA
reminding myself no two flakes are the same.

Wondering if there were times my mother was
so stumped by the cold she pondered the faeries

what they might consider a fair swap.

In This Photo I Am on the Cusp

Thirteen years old, just before we made the move
from suburban to rural biases, from Catholic single-sex
to state co-ed.
Before my first kiss set the bar to science fiction
and I stopped telling my mother everything.

We are five siblings abreast and I am harpooned
by love for us all.

For myself, having recently outgrown a bowlish haircut
trying to set myself apart, still holding out hope
I could change the world before it changed me.

The only boy, who people often mistake
in this photo for another sister, twiggy legs
shooting free of frayed denim shorts, the pantomime
grin, hand extending a badminton racquet across
our descending line trying to barricade the silliness
a few years more. Our heads tilted inward
as if in a prescient nod to the kindred spirits we
would discover in each other much later, too briefly.

The middle child for a few weeks more slanting
a dark fringe and clutching a doll like a life preserver.
Already she looks determined to save every wild and hunted thing.

The next, even then with a half-formed smile covering
a slight overlap of teeth, unaware of her power
her hibernating swan-beauty.

Tapered at the end in a turtle neck
green as the Ireland she would be the only one of us
to return to for good, our little envoy.

Somewhere out of shot Mum ready to pop
out the last scallywag girl destined to spark
a firecracker light through all our ages.

And Dad, perhaps behind the camera, gob-smacked
by a burgeoning female brood he hadn't counted on
all those years ago off ship beguiled by the spirit
of an Aussie barmaid and the allure of a fresh start
where his accent would be more a charm
than any kind of deep seeded threat.

The Word Itself

We are first shaped by love through the senses,
the nearness and farness of everything.

*You dragged your casted legs behind you happy
as Larry* says my mother glass half full.

The word itself at some point
gaining hope-fuelled weight illuminating
the importance of timing a smile.
The enticing win win of reciprocity.

Good luck to you then says my father meaning
I love you too.

Discovering The Kiss then the real thing
(as luck would have it) no less disappointing
rounding edges and encouraging belief beyond
the mere physics of breathing underwater.

You are the only girl I ever really dug says my first
boyfriend in a letter long after I'd moved past
that once upon a time.

Shaped further by taste and obsession
by dogged friendships and obscure causes.

I tell my sister *You became the favourite
part of the trinity our parents needed to survive
death's most grievous error.*

Through imitation and invention, covenant and betrayal.

I am not coming home says my husband over the phone.

Always at the centre of our shape-shifting the same small
echo chamber, the same bewildering space we call heart
and soul ... and sometimes God.

To the Householder

Because it is Halloween
and I am in the wrong hemisphere
or because the moon is almost full again,
or because news of the death of an old lover
reminds me there will be others;
and if I had thought about this then
there might have been more,
or simply because I am new to the neighbourhood
and it is stamped and handwritten
I open the letter addressed to The Householder
calling me to Heaven on Earth.

Part of me knows it makes good business sense,
hedging a bet I might read and dismiss
but not so readily throw out the word of any god.

That I might try to pinpoint exactly when it was
I stopped praying in the ways I was taught,
and started resurrecting faces from the shadows
just to ask for directions.

All Souls' Day

Offerings, kitsch as
the Sacred Heart's 7 watts.

Mouths, soul-shaped,
singing each other into being,
dancing the dirt back into stardust.

It cannot be overdone
this welcoming home.

So ...

a truckload of snuff for my granny,
a black pudding pinwheel
and a jug of Lourdes water to wash it down.

For Nana light beer on tap,
a transistor radio, racing form guides
and a bottomless box
of diabetic dark chocolate covered ginger.

For my hippy brother
who put his own dogs down,
when it came to it,
but could not rest easy
in a room with a spider,
who said he wouldn't live
past forty and didn't:
cheese blocks and pickle jars,
a trail of hemp seeds
to find his way.

For my polio-stunted aunt
who missed her calling,
expertly drawing on her eyebrows
so that she had the permanent look
of an eternal optimist:

travel brochures
and a library of unabridged,
choose your own
adventure, romance novels.

For the littlest one of us
a single lungful of air,
just enough to be born with,
to know the sweet and sour
of what it is to live
against the skin of the world.

Liberty

I see now, forty years on,
I had no business running away.

My own motherhood since
showing me the insult of a note
that reads *don't worry*
as if it was a choice.

Though we never understood disposable
and equated adulthood with privilege,
eyeing off Dad's piece of fish
as we counted the number
of chips on each sibling's plate,
my concept of liberty was righteous.

Once when I had the farm to myself
I wedged the shed doors wide open
encouraging the chickens to leave,
sixteen thousand of them,
huddled wing to useless wing,
each blinking three sets of eyelids
into the alien light.

Maybe I believed enough children
after me would make up the difference
but it doesn't work that way does it?
Each one has a part of you
that cannot be replicated
and I will never know what did
and didn't grow in my absence.

What a long-time lesson it is
that we are both diminished
and extended by family.

That our time here is governed
by such imagined freedoms,

that hold our hearts to ransom,
that would have us believe
love can be selective and conditional ...
and still be love.

Recalibration

If I had enough faith, I would invoke Saint Cuthbert
to find and count and bring home every last, lost sheep.
Even those who believe themselves to be first,
to be already found.

While outside a neighbour's front gate
a cardboard box and a sign reading *free lemons*.
Once coveted fruit of ancient Rome, now common as tears.
I take three, leave a smile at the window
and this small act of reciprocity
somehow marks the day for balance,
temporarily misting the sharp edges
and sheer drops
which present themselves often enough
wrenching some of us out of time,
tempting others irrevocably turned
by unfathomable wounding.

Inside these citrus skins
lies the gift of transformation.

I'm thinking gelatinous cheesecake,
dreamy peaks of meringue
and that old family favourite ...
Lemon Delicious Pudding,
for its magic shape-shifting,
its delicate, stupefying comfort.

In the end I simply squeeze the juice
into mugs of hot water, add honey
and let the old ways lay their claims;
inevitable seasonal shifts
recalibrating the sum of my parts.

Guises

The truly fateful ones
are not surgical, or layered
in paper mache.
Not framed in fur and feathers.
Do not attract penalties
or chime and glint
their myriad distractions.

They are the ones we assume
over a lifetime of trying
to stand out or blend in.
Affected and practised
to the point of acceptance.

It has been thus for so long now.
We have all but forgotten what it is
to be naked before our gods
who surely ache in their loneliness
to be inspired once more
by the raw and exquisite shock of us.

Introductions

Twenty years on I confess
exaggerating myself when we met
for fear of being overlooked.

Suggesting a photographic memory
unlimited expense account
and an intimate knowledge of all things
purple.

Only that last claim was genuine
in its awkward attempt at truth.

Here are some of the facts:

My birthstone is amethyst.

At age thirteen I was mixing red and blue
in art class when a girl I hardly knew
(niece to one of the nuns) tapped me
on the shoulder, slapping the novice from my face.

Every Sunday over the football season
the new priest's stole, rallied with team colours
so that trust came easily and we
were blinded to the mortal sins of the Father.

The mulberry tree was laden
when my children's father-to-be
forked his teenage tongue around mine,
kissing me a message I chose to ignore,
introducing me to the sounds of rock
knocking on my back door.

I do not think I have favourite shades
until I close my eyes and hear them:

Byzantium, heliotrope, thistle,
long distance, pompadour...

See how uncomplicated love can be?

If I were to introduce myself to you now
I would not bother to mention such vanities
as two hundred and fifty thousand sea snails
boiling in lead vats to procure a single ounce
of dye. The extravagant stench.

I would simply point out
the possibilities of us – elapsing.
Warn against nostalgia
and money's false-positive.
Promise to make you laugh and cry
and laugh again.

Fairy Tales from the Future

It happens so gradually it's easy to forget
we are living the science fiction of the past,
where only madmen and women soliloquised.

Now anyone can be witnessed in passionate discourse,
cutting the business deal of their career mid-air,
parting crowds with entitled stares.

Washing machines sing end of cycle tunes:
Responding to smart phones in smart homes,
responding to programmed chips worn like corsages
as isolated bodies repeat unrequited moves.

Even tea leaves in a bag
were once the stuff of make-believe.

How odd, how thrilling to think
what the fairy tales of the future might hold:
An ozone layer that needed protection.
Gender politics and hate crime.
Animal rights and elder abuse.
Poets incarcerated for doing the soul's work.
The soul itself quantified at 21 grams, weighing in
at more than the African pygmy mouse
but significantly less than a light bulb.

Incognito

It was chance and a neat trick
discovering that spot on my bedroom floor
where the radio reception changed with
one stamp of the foot, one twitch of the nose.

Just enough to convince my neighbour,
the wannabe witch, I was the real deal.
Of course, she'd worked it out by our next playdate
with the help of her science-minded parents
who attended the other church.

But we kept up the pretence, choosing to stay
for as long as we could under cover of childhood.
We tucked our tails and flexed our wings.
All beguiling smiles and nursery rhymes.
A slow burn rising out of place and time.

The Lore of Poetry

Behind a blur of Bunsen burners, my mid-teens
could find rhythm and rhyme in any formula.

No justification of changing properties
ever improved my science grade.

Then one day my lab partner,
the most timid girl in class,
admitted heartache equally weighted
between thoughts of dissection
and my poems.

And this was it. The cause and effect
I'd been looking for, thought I understood ...

Much later learning it is not enough
to move the easily moved.
That testing is a matter of trial and mistrial.

Of disappointing those with hopeful stares
awaiting translation or a punchline or both.
Enraging the naysayers who insist
certain key elements have been overlooked
or plagiarised.

Hardest to bear, perhaps, the ones who blush
against implication as if some carefully hidden self
had been publicly and unfairly revealed.

But there will always be a handful
who feel the seismic shift, for whom the lore
of poetry will make sudden, inarticulate sense.

Discovering Iris

The boys drag their early teens
through the streets,
camouflaged in uniforms
they'll soon slake off.
They're talking about Iris
or one of them
is trying to make a point,
trying to illuminate memory.

You know Iris? he begins ...
Blank stares, shoulder shrugs.
He tries again
separating the two syllables
of her name slowly
so as not to damage the whole –
I   ris?

No response.
Perhaps the old fashioned
has thrown them.
Now Brianna or Madison ...
but Iris?
Like an eye? Like the flower?

*Iris from school, from the skate park,
from last night* he prods.

They're oblivious, disinterested
and he can't understand it because
to him *Iris is everywhere* ...
then he too falls silent, shakes his head
as the realization sinks in.
Some boyhood discoveries can't be shared.
Not when there's nothing.
Not when there's no one
to compare.

What Hope Did We Have?

between art and the confessional?
Of course we expected sparks from life.

Summertime,
that Hepburn-Brazzi kiss
imprinted against a night sky
of fireworks set the bar
addictively out of reach.

I read Fahrenheit 451
in slow motion
as if it was the last book
and I the last reader.

You took bit parts on stage
and let the devil have his say.

All this ...

and yet, how to explain what incited us
the day we burned each other out.

How we could never have withdrawn
from those particular personal flames
without turning each love letter from ash
to char back to the dear heart's
guileless composition, without acknowledging
all that was flammable between us
smoulders still...

In His Way

He would go to his grave having never laid a hand
on any one of them. Not once.

Not the son who anesthetized his own meanness
into a softness that would eventually sink him.

Not the too many daughters
who grew to outrun and outsmart him.

Not even when he saw the way other men
looked at his wife, the way she looked back,
the wounding, unintelligible language of their smiles.

No, not even then.

There were times he knew they thought him monstrous,
never saw how short the leash was.

When things got too close, he closed himself off,
head bowed before chisel and lathe.

In his way he tried to mend every broken thing
they left at his door.

If only life could be shaped just so.
If only less could really be more.

Family Traits

My mother and I share two slightly webbed toes
while her brother's are fully fused.
When I ask where they come from
she confesses from Great-Uncle Donald,
illegitimate son of Count Duckula.
Humour and silver linings
have always paved her way.

My own way began with feet crossing the threshold
between worlds well before the heart, the head;
snowflakes sacrificing their uniqueness
to piles of sameness against hospital walls
while somewhere close by
my father, up to his neck in blarney,
avoiding a speeding ticket.

I am not one for team sports
or gymnasium mirrors but I can walk
until the cows run away from home.
It is my chosen form of therapy.

When my hip was replaced
and I could not reach to clip my toenails
the pedicure my daughter gave me
played its part in healing
all that had stretched
and threatened to split between us.

I like to think mermaids and selkies
are rife in our family sagas
but adjoining digits are no more mystical
than they are new.

It turns out I could just as easily be part seagull
part tree frog, part kangaroo...

Small Offerings

On a fair day I'm a tree hugger,
at least in theory,
but not a sitter
or any kind of foot soldier.
I cannot tell
one battlefield from another.

Easily overcome by statistics on countries
most dangerous, most peaceful -
from El Salvador to Iceland.
My own birth country today
reaching 50,000 Covid deaths.
My father's neighbouring land
still menaced by the threat
of violent regression.

And the faraway place we choose
to call home with its brutal history
so whitewashed that I read
the Martu have no word for warfare.
Who is there left to question
but myself and my god?
What is there left to do but continue
to make these small offerings of poems,
killing my darlings until motive is clear.

Though I Whispered Subliminal Poetry

from a young age, my daughters always had
a pistol grip on the world's edge.
Each flirted with frills and the soft centred,
but also the boxing bag, target archery.
And swordplay, favouring épée,
where no body part was out of bounds.

As the years slip, almost unseen into the decades,
I witness in them such fortitude,
such actualised potential that I sometimes wonder
if they adopted me.

Mother's Day gifts of potpourri
fortified into toolboxes,
flashlights, keychains with compasses
and safety whistles attached.
I suspect these days
they each have within easy reach
a bug-out bag packed for a moment's notice,
that they swap tips on surviving the zombie apocalypse,
ask each other what to do about Mum.

I do not want to worry them but, it's true enough,
the more they mature the more I seem to regress.

I make promises, we know, I struggle to keep:
Not to leave my phone at home. Don't talk to strangers.
Don't walk alone in the park trusting the dark to shield me.

Not to wander off without a plan,
never mind a final destination.

To the Hitchhiker

Far from dog walking in suburbia,
your backpack looks light enough
to suggest intent but only half a plan.
Thumb angled for a lift,
you catch my eye at highway speed
and I do not stop.

I think about you on and off
the rest of the day remembering my daughters
and their post-apocalyptic leanings.
How I begged them not to hitchhike
because I did, and almost didn't
get away with it.
Though I don't explain this
until they are past listening
and will be who they will be.

But you have your Pit Bull
and that's something right?
Whether you kept man's best friend
on a short leash or learned from him
how to follow your own nose home.

Chances are we will never meet.
I will never know the story of your journey.

If your bag was full of bones and 2 minute noodles.
If you believed in Occam's Razor, guardian angels.

If you had someone waiting for your return or arrival
ready to speak your name in such a way
that you would desire nothing more than to stay.

Gold

Chewing pine resin and adorning myself
with garlands of Capeweed,
I was in love with the uncultivated.
With found objects, real and imagined,
from Venus flytraps to Triffids.

The landscaped garden often confused me
with its maze of hedges
and coordinated groupings
of analogous colours.

Surrounded by bouquets of eucalyptus
I grew up with a predilection
for peppermint and lemon over rose and lily.

Flowering alongside the dinosaurs.
Adapting to resprout after fire and drought.
Learning to protect themselves against attack.
Changing scent from one side to the other.

I am only mildly surprised to learn
X-rays have shown traces of gold in gum leaves
and that one woman chose to spend 449 days,
60 metres up, honouring and protecting
- breathe in, breathe out -
the life that enables ours.

In Hindsight

which is the opposite of second-sight
and takes decades of growing pains,
I would not be silent as my schoolmates joked
about the boy whose father died in a manner
belying even the shadiest sense of humour.

I would have held the lover I was leaving
who had already left me, whose betrayal was crippling
but who needed, in that moment more than forgiveness,
more than breath itself, to be held.

Some days we struggle with the smallest act
of goodwill, so caught up in the net
of our own desire to be seen through.

Other days we are humbled by flickers
of insight into the human milieu
encouraging us to forgive old hurts
and our part in them.
Recognise the fear behind the rage.
The loneliness driving the worst kind
of relationship.

We are dying, all of us.
And maybe none of it
is being tallied up:
an eye for an eye, dust to dust.

But maybe it is,
and kindness is the only equaliser we have,
the sole measure of our collective worth.

Milk Moon

starless night
the phone stop-starts my heart.
I try the name on for size
granny

milk moon
the mother
my daughter
will become
acknowledging
the light and shadow
of each phase

snail path
her mindful steps
first trimester
I remember this heightened
sense of everything

hand on belly
how the world curves
toward her
every move deepens
their connection

first strokes
of my grandchild's face
twelve-week scan
in my dreams we colour in
outside the lines

the cat yowls
at the bedroom door
third trimester
the day-long hours
come and go

mother nature
exercising the body
Braxton-Hicks
the textbooks
tell half the story

waters break
suddenly determined
to finish the sandwich
memorising flavour and texture
pre-parenthood

in labour her cries for help
penetrate my every cell
for a moment
our worlds collapse
then they rise

skin on skin
the word miracle overused
still my head bows
a silent prayer echoing
generations

wildflowers
this year I see another colour
spring baby
you are here you are here
as if you are the first

in my arms
daughter of my daughter
the old songs
returning one by one
we begin again

Writing the Light

I can no more write the light
than I can paint or dance it,
but tonight the last of it haloes
stratocumulus clouds as if
God has skipped rose gold pebbles
across the glass floor of heaven.

And isn't it there, also,
in the waves that form shadows.
In both the heart of the inferno
and its dying embers.
Inside the giant bubbles
the busker lassoes into life
beneath the souvenir shop.
Along the deepest creases
of old wedding polaroids.
In the spark in my grandchild's eyes
testing all our futures.

Meditation for the World-Weary
after 'Landscape and jacaranda' by Grace Cossington Smith

Here is a grass bed; sap green.
Lie down and allow the day to unwind you
as aromatics shift and drift a single petal
to cradle your world-weary head.

Each stroke of the scene
mellows to hold you
until you are ready
to re-enter the world, tabula rasa.

Here, take from the dream tree
this seedling to breathe by.

Dog with Girl
after 'Girl with dog' by Joy Hester

Remember us this way -
aligned together in strokes of slumber
our panting slowed to rhythmic
breathing hair and skin
no longer mistress and hound
but somehow made kin
by our shared and simple dreaming
by this wish to remain hybrid companions
until we are each called by name
as the sun lips the edge of the world
and we slip our shadows without trace
and all things being equal give chase ...

How I Come to Know You

Back when I was mother superior
and you were my devotee,
blind to my parenthood painting by numbers,
you wore stuck-on tattoos and clip-on earrings.

Your best friend was an Australorp named Blacky.
Your white-blonde hair could not be tamed –
directionless as a chook's bum on a windy day.

When Simon our goat was killed and curried,
you gave thanks, ate him with reverence
and embraced vegetarianism as religion.

Your treasures included
a rock n' roll doll and a toy dump truck.
Once, you calmed a stray Rottweiler
to eat from your hand.

When you moved into Teenage-hood
the clip-ons were found wanting.
You suggested a piercer.
I insisted a doctor, held your hand
and looked elsewhere
until the needle drew a cry from us both.

Post infection I understood the lesson.
Piercers specialize, Mum, GP's generalize.

Now your body is a kaleidoscope
of keepsakes and talismans.
You tell me there is a story behind each image.

The goldfish, the jester hat, anchors and hearts,
cups and teapots, even guns and knives
have their part to play in *all that jazz.*
A four leaf clover and a small star
guide you through the brincled nights.

Between Breaths

This is how I come to know you
(my) tattooed, pierced, rainbow haired, vegan,
gender-neutral-identifying,
ineffable grown-up child.

How I am become your number one fan.

Some Thoughts on Red

after remembering a girl with dandelion seed hair
the way her voice rose with her blush.

Thoughts on red continue:

What my father saw in those moments
instead of the faces of his children.

Overcompensating
the dachshund's studded collar.

The colour of the sound of sirens.

Underneath my tiny thumb scar,
rivers of sisterhood.

Lambrusco and the promises it couldn't keep.

Between lives, beating softly against the window,
that robin's breast.

Makers

I knew a man whose ex took years
to knit him out of her system
all those dropped stiches and do overs.

We are all makers.
Each breath priming the air for the next.

My great aunt –
celestial scone maker, piano player
outdid herself with intricate motifs,
her thick-framed spectacles
magnifying the trifles
of idyllic country scenes.

I admired her fingers,
in perpetual motion,
but was smitten by
the delicate line of moustache,
the careful arrangement
of a lilac tinted hairdo.

A childhood friend gathered and spun
moulted hair from her cherished Persian.

And my own hands,
restless with unmade poems,
turning to layettes
in my sister's final weeks.

The rainbow wool I used to fashion
a strange animal companion
I imagined all too easily my nephew
dribbling over, teething on.
Naming and keeping.
The rosy thread of smile
he would surely return again and again.

Between Breaths

I see now in the photograph
how purposefully it is anchored
under the curve of his arm
against the dear stopped heart of him.

Guardian of dreams.
Of unknowable lives
.

The Ghost of Maria Goretti Speaks

The day I opened the door
in my parent's absence to Alessandro,
whose longing I understood
to be misguided as my own,
was only the beginning.

Yes, we fought and he the stronger;
the blade striking me once
for every station of the cross,
letting more of my blood and faith
than I could hope to live without.

On my deathbed
I bestowed an absolution
born of instinct not instruction.
We are all other until we are not.

I have watched the story twist and turn,
tendrils of witch's smoke
through the silencing ages
as young girls add my name
and those of my virgin martyr sisters
to their own.

Generations of child-brides
intent on goodness being
the simple subtraction
of right from wrong.

The truth is I haunted him
hungrily, artlessly.

My sainthood shocked us both.

Blooming in the Dark

Each year six stockings
stretched to capacity with trinkets:
yoyos, puzzles, bangles, crayons,
matchbox cars and marbles
sourced throughout the year.

The exact same number of things in each.
At the bottom always an orange.
At the top a book and a balloon
perfectly paired
in the secret knowledge
held by all bibliophiles
that reading is synonymous with floating.

One Christmas Eve
was spent sewing a new outfit
for each favoured doll
and love-worn bear,
even GI Joe got a makeover.

My mother was by all accounts
no great seamstress, cook or crafter
but could turn her hand to any of it
blooming like an evening primrose
in the dark after prayers,
encouraging us to dream
of time-warped kisses.
Other selves in other realms…

The Other Side

I never understood
the constant implicit
in happily-ever-afters.

I yearned for sequels and prequels.
Alternate paths linking dualities.
A spotlight on bestial beauty
and the deliberate underdog.

I wanted to know the other side
of every story.

I confess my heart was torn between
Dopey and Bashful.
The loneliness of the wolf
and the hunger of the witch.

Some days,
I could not see the glitter
for the cinders.

But the moon
was always hung
low and protective
above my delicate
chicken legged home ...
and Baba Yaga was just a name,
sweet as any.

Play

Once, after a prolonged losing streak
you took a three-year hiatus from the game.
I tried every combination of letters
but could not persuade you back to the board.

Instead, I'd catch you off guard
as we strolled through parklands
say suddenly - Close your eyes
and count to twenty! - knowing you
owed me this much.

Hidden, I watched as you stood there,
a man in sore need of a haircut
the papery end of sixty, face in hands
numbering backwards
as couples and dogs skirted about you
and children too sometimes
blinking recognition, due respect
for the primal majesty of play.

Today Was Inconsolable

and all the old comforts fell short:
fish and chips, Stark Trek,
a walk along the riverbank.

The hot water bottle cooled too quickly.

The guided meditation was interrupted
by calls of nature and something
I'd left on the stove.

Even dredging up memories
of the blind masseur felt tainted.

But the day is now being flattered
by the night in such sure and trusting strokes.
And there is that chapbook I just bought
entitled Twelve Poems about Chickens
which makes me wonder
how many of them
thought the sky was falling
and just thinking that,
just writing it down
brings me close enough to the border
between catch and release.

The Spark

Some of us believe
by a certain age it's finite.
While others continue
to flicker & flame.

This woman for instance,
the morse code
of her oversized handbag
bling reflecting summer.

Just shy of the zebra
crossing, sprinting
a closing gap
in the two-way traffic.
Eyes fixed
on the other side
calculating risk
not quite playing chicken.

Each multi-faceted sequin
winking the same clear message:

Not yet, not yet, not yet.

The Gap

Because no none would speak of him –

the father you were too young to recall meeting
before his leaving –

Your whole life you have not known
where they came from
those characteristics of your youth
unshared with half-siblings:

Gesticulating hands and feet
that generated their own beat.
A reporter's ear for melodrama
and a desire to coax the truth from it.
Coppered skin and inkjet hair.
Hazel eyes searching vainly
for the man you imagined opened
then closed your mother's heart.

Once, you heard from a distant in-law
that he had only three loves:
The music. The drink. The women.
That was it. As if to say more
would be irresponsibly gratuitous.

Who could blame you then
for trying to fill the gap,
allowing your eyelids to close
against swirling hues of sepia –
from the mahogany, spruce and cedar
of acoustic guitars
to amber beer on tap,
to the stockinged legs of Garbo
before the talkies discredited
all belief.

Dream Analysis 101

Perhaps it is the dream
I should be lying on my therapist's couch
to tell and even then telling it
as belonging to a friend whose psyche
I am holding for safe keeping ...

But here we are.

I am being chased by a work in progress,
a definition-seeking skeleton if you will.

As is the way with such dreams,
picking up pace only slows me down.
With each brief glance
chanced across my left shoulder
the more fleshed-out my pursuer becomes
and the less ground I have gained.

It is a lengthy process this becoming.

Linking tributaries of blood,
fusing shards of bone,
ascending to the face
where whorls of emotion
hold and lose their shape
in that singular, particular way
I almost fail to recognise as my own.

Redefining Romance

I confess I've had my nauseating even noxious
    moments
but it was never cut flowers I desired

bunched in cellophaned body bags
    dissolving
aspirin to keep them fresh one day longer

while currents of distress ran beneath our feet
    seeking
so much more than the romance of the ages

the unfolding of each unwritten day into lived story
    faith
the satin bowerbird's promised bits of sky

My Relationship with Food

is complicated.
I go to the shops for oven cleaner
and return with ice cream.

When I tell my mother this she says
when I was cutting my first teeth
one atypical cloudless morning
(the day before pay day),
stuck fast in a corner of her purse
a single coin allocated
for sandwich filling.
Something healthy.

Instead,
we shared a cone of soft serve
in the park
the sun melting time
and transgression.

Back home,
two slices of bread,
buttered and sugared
as if we were on holiday
instead of saving
for the Lucky Country.

A decade on Dad's T-bone steak
is damned to hell and back,
tough as old boots
and Mum's expressions
begin to turn inward, though never fully.

I am the same kind of optimistic cook
as my maternal forebears –
tweaking the plainest, most frugal dish
until it becomes a guessing game
which part of the world it's from.

Between Breaths

My grandmother's Christmas puddings
were heavy on the sherry and lard,
hung in rows from the garage rafters
until skins formed
intoxicated and thick enough
to withstand any fault line.

When the stroke felled her
leeching the mischief from her eyes
I could not get enough of the scent
of steaming fruit pudding –
anything proportionally fat and sweet.

Intuited

1/

A gridlock of potential
waiting for the lights to change.
Window down, arm out.
The analogue clock
tattooed on her bicep,
hands set to commemorate.
Only when the right muscle
is flexed is it time to move on.

2/

In the crowded café the theatre
of their newly dyed hair
is expertly distracting,
faces unreadable as drought.
A depth of friendship hinted at
in mirrored composure –
the way one voice discreetly
hums over the tremors.

3/

Still owning the streets
in hipster jeans
ready to outstare the critics,
young and unambiguous
as I once was.
The tight white t-shirt
late-stage pregnancy,
a full moon in-your-face cliché.
Unasked for but intuited,
some kind of blessing
just crossed my path.

Out for the Count

It was as if someone finally noticed
the class clown had a gun.

And the pack moved in
as well it should have done.

But the fear behind the fear persists.

That we are estranged now even more.
Understand each other even less.

No Thanks but in the Giving

In acknowledging the sorrow
that doubles the joy.
The shadow that sanctions the light.

Each of life's potholes
stumbled into and out of
before coming upon
the next promising bend in the path.

Parents of course
whose euphemisms for love
are rare found objects
useless to anyone else's children.
My dad's *good luck to you then*
Mum's failsafe recipe for chocolate
self-saucing pudding.

Sisters who just are.
Without whom I would be
less known to myself.

A brother who ignited
fury and compassion
then left and left until
there could be no returning
but through the eyes of doppelgängers.

Children who mimic and mock
only to reflect kindly,
at times wisely
turning as they must
into their own unique version of themselves.

Friends who see through neediness
to pure ungraspable grace.
Memory-making with the one I choose.
Who chooses me.
To guard against

becoming strangers
while understanding
there is no such guard.

Elders who say
they have all the time in the world.

Even this shaky faith
beating its ancient recalcitrant heart
trusting sporadically
in all that is unquantifiable:
Invisible threads and mends.
Earth-quaking butterflies.
Tidal shifts making good on their promise
night after night to keep me buoyed.

Now You Think You Have Learned

what it is to be patient,
to sit by the window
and watch the play of light
against time.

You tell yourself there can be no place
for the rioting mind, the stagnant heart
now the air is breathable
and the waterways almost persuasive with life.
That your first steps must count
as if they are being counted.

One morning
you will leave the imposition of your home,
reacquaint yourself with the streets
by nodding each neighbour's house
back into being,
naming the names you know,
once more promising yourself
to learn the others.

You might stay out all day all night,
reacquaint yourself with the whole suburb.
Visit your favourite barista or book seller.
Play tourist or home-coming queen.

Keep going.
Venture into those parts of the city
you'd only seen from the inside of a taxi.

Discover the people there
were sheltered for a while
but grew restless, suspicious
and when the worst was thought to be over,
chose to return to the streets
as if they had unfinished business.

Between Breaths

When they make eye contact
it will take everything
you think you have learned
not to be the first to look away.

This Prodigious Life

Once I wanted nothing less
than the face of Jesus
baked into a girl guide biscuit.

No amount of triangulating –
ethos, pathos, logos –
ever showed me
the path to faith.
It just was.
It just is.

When I learn the term sacred bombing
I understand nothing but language as the enemy.
As everything anti.

Miracles are not multiples of loaves and fishes
but a single continuum of breath.

I've known people who emerge from silent retreats
as if they have discovered the secret
but cannot share it in words.

They walk through their muted sun-kissed lives
for as long as we allow it.
Sometimes longer.

Others for whom every day is a magic trick
and a willingness to believe
is all that keeps them from folding.

I am not named after anyone
but when I look it up,
God is gracious. God is merciful.
my cup runneth over.

Author Profile

Jane Williams was born in England in 1964 and is based in Tasmania, Australia. Since the early 1990s her poems have been published in most major Australian literary journals and newspapers, in periodicals and online in countries including Ireland, USA, Canada, England, Japan, Sweden and India She is the author of five books of poetry and a collection of stories. While best known for her poetry she enjoys writing across forms and genres, for children and in collaboration with other artists. She has read her poetry in USA, Canada, Ireland, England, Malaysia, Czech Republic and Slovakia where she held a three month residency in 2016. Awards for her poetry include the Anne Elder Award, the D.J. O'Hearn Memorial Fellowship and the Bruce Dawe Prize.

www.ingramcontent.com/pod-product-compliance
Lightning Source LLC
Chambersburg PA
CBHW062155100526
44589CB00014B/1846